THE UNYIELDING WEIGHT OF
WORDS

To those who paint pictures of hope and love
by carefully choosing their words,
in the belief that everyone deserves respect.

Jacalyn Eyvonne

THE UNYIELDING WEIGHT OF WORDS

Jacalyn Eyvonne

Poems for Reflection, Healing, and Love

The Unyielding Weight of Words
Poems for Reflection, Healing, and Love

Cover Design, NeuImagery, Neuman Robinson
Interior Art Photography by Jacalyn Eyvonne
www.jacalyneyvonne.com

ISBN: 979-8-9895050-0-5 - Paperback
ISBN: 979-8-9895050-1-2 - Hardcover
ISBN: 979-8-9895050-2-9 - eBook
First Edition – January 2024
SoulStanzas Books
JE Books, Vallejo, CA

Library of Congress Control Number: 2023922960

Content Page

The wounds of words can linger long after they are gone.

Jacalyn Eyvonne

Preface

The rain that day reflected the pain in my heart as racist and hurtful words washed over me like a vicious, relentless storm. I could not help but feel the deluge was an omen, a warning of the tumultuous journey ahead. But from that moment of darkness, a fire burned within me.

Words have an incredible power to shape our world. What we say and hear can profoundly affect our lives, from how we communicate with others to our beliefs about ourselves and society. We've all experienced moments where a harsh comment or an insult has pierced us deeply. But the effects of unfriendly words run deeper than hurt feelings. Negative language can damage a person's self-esteem, making them doubt their worth and potential. They can build a person up or tear them down, leading to internalizing defeatist thoughts and depression or anxiety. Inappropriate comments can leave deep scars on a person's psyche. They can be long-lasting and take significant effort to heal.

Consider a child experiencing discouraging language; children are like sponges; they absorb everything around them, including how we speak. The language a child hears can profoundly affect their emotional development.

Racism is one of the most significant social issues plaguing today. It dehumanizes people, reduces them to a mere group rather than individuals with worth, and restricts them from their full potential. Racism explicitly degrades and insults the dignity of others based on skin color or any other physical, social, or cultural characteristics. Hostile speech or slurs enhance the disparity felt by those affected by it. All of which can have a butterfly effect on the community. Fostering a culture of intolerance, division, and hate makes moving forward and creating a more welcoming and equal society even harder.

Society is a complex structure of individuals, and words play a significant role in shaping it. The impact can be far-reaching when people become easily influenced by marginalizing behavior.

With the proliferation of social media, aggressive discourse can quickly spread, influencing a broader audience and creating a vicious cycle of denigratory communication. Negative words can lead to social stratification, discrimination, and exclusion. Therefore, it is crucial to be mindful of what we say and how it affects society. We all are responsible for positively impacting the world, starting with our utterances. Using words that lift people instead of tearing them down can create a more inclusive and harmonious society.

In "The Unyielding Weight of Words," I delve deeper into the impact of words in our society through the lens of poetry. Exploring love and hate, homelessness, ageism, choice, and hope, examining moments of joy and beauty to the pain and struggles endured. It provides a poignant reflection on our society's need for empathy, love, and compassion. It is a powerful reminder of the incredible impact that our words can have.

Within each chapter, the focus is on specific themes. For example, I highlight different facets under the love category, from the euphoric feeling of falling in love to the heart-wrenching pain of unrequited love. I also delve deeper into the various forms of love - the kind between family, friends, and oneself.

The collection raises provocative questions about the source and consequences of hate and invites the reader to consider how hate manifests in our society. Through its intense and visceral language, the poems voice the rage, frustration, and sadness of experiencing or witnessing hatred.

Homelessness highlights the stark reality of life on the streets and the challenges of trying to survive in a world that can be cruel and unyielding. It examines the sobering perspective of the impact of homelessness, often influenced by systemic societal inequities.

While I explored Ageism through all aspects of life, from the workplace to our relationships, through poetic verse, words delve deep into how ageism contributes to a less compassionate society and the biases attached to growing old.

In conclusion, "The Unyielding Weight of Words" is a collection of poetry that tackles the most pressing issues of our time. The book's themes are universal, and I present my poems in a way that opens new avenues of thought and analysis.

I am grateful to everyone who embarked on this poetic journey with me. Hopefully, "The Unyielding Weight of Words" touches your heart, stirs your soul, and moves you emotionally. Leaving an indelible imprint upon your mind as each page reminds us of our humanity.

I remember the chilling memory of the day I stood drenched in the rain, the moment I first encountered racism, remains permanently etched in my mind. It serves as a reminder of how it feels to be assaulted by hurtful comments and the pain discrimination and bigotry can cause. It has also taught me that poetry can heal and that our words have the incredible power to shape a better world.

The Power of a Word

Words can be weapons that scar,
cutting through flesh and bone
leaving unhealed wounds.
Where a single phrase can weaken
or hold power to start a war.
Through the ages, their echo resonates,
shattering the broken for a lifetime.
In a world so often filled with darkness,
our tongues should be instruments of peace,
where joy mends and soothes like a
gentle breeze, bringing the hearts of the
world closer than they were before.

Jacalyn Eyvonne

LOVE

CHAPTER 1

Jacalyn Eyvonne

The Breath of You

Though fragile
hearts quiver
knowing that
true love
is not free of pain.
My fears have
scattered by the
breath of you
the delicate touches
and expressions of
emotions cultivated.
Beside you
I am exposed
and vulnerable
yet I am nourished
eternally.

Sweet Smell of Passion

The air is thick with a sweet smell of passion,
as two hearts beat beneath diamond raindrops,
cascading from above.

The sky cries with tears to bring hope to the gloom,
tenderly intertwined with a fountain of love
falling upon soulful kisses, nurtured,
and protected under the descent, droplets of affection,
spirited by the beauty of what nature presents.

Hearts Harmony

It's hard to hear our voices amid the chaos when light and darkness merge. The notes of pain and frustration intermingle, creating an internal clamor that threatens to drown out our love for one another. Battles easily break out amid trying times, casting a shadow over what we have shared.

However, in such moments, we must remember the importance of finding the eternal balance of love that weaves throughout our hearts. We must fight against the strains of life that threaten to pull us apart and instead find the love where our two hearts can harmonize.

It is loving that leaves behind only beauty, a song to sing across the affection shared. It is love that is eternal, the thing, that feeling we must hold dear and never let go. Love defines us, makes us who we are, and guides us toward the harmony and happiness we seek.

You Are My Light

You are the soft
petals falling
into my hand,
the light that
escapes the sky
spreading across
this vast land.
The endless nights
and breaking dawn,
my certainty,
amidst uncertainty,
my enduring love.
An offering of honesty
beneath a poetic
incandescent moon.
You are the one
that has healed
all my wounds.

Love Blaze

Anger's fire may scorch and sear
like a blaze of embers smoldering
with an intensity unlike any other.
Love can melt away the icy barriers
put up to protect us from the world.
It radiates warmth and kindness,
filling us with a sense of harmony
that no other emotion can match.
When love takes hold, it transforms,
opening avenues of creativity
and constructive collaboration
that we never thought possible.
It ignites our passions and fuels our desires,
bringing us together in an unbreakable,
undeniable bond.

Let love blaze within you and be your guide, unstoppable,
Unyielding. Watch as it burns through the darkness,
illuminating your path toward a brighter tomorrow.

Hidden Hope

Emotions shrouded in complexity make it easy to feel
your mind growing brittle as the weight of it all bears
down upon you. Passing moments where splinters of hate
reveal themselves, parading their silhouettes through the
restless cities as anger and ugliness reign supreme. It is
easy to feel you are drowning in a sea of misery where the
light of hope seems to stray away.

Yet, amid ugliness, strength and tenderness lie within
every soul. Sometimes, it lurks dormant, waiting and
yearning to reveal and unfold, to replace the scars of the
past with the bright fires of passion that still burn within.
Even in the darkest moments, hope still glimmers, hidden
away within the dimness of sorrow and despair.

Knowing that we all carry this hidden hope through the
darkest times becomes a humbling realization.
A reminder that even when the world feels like it is
crushing us beneath its weight, there is still a glimmer of
light waiting to be uncovered. The darkness surrounding
us must not dishearten but move us to look forward with
hope and trust in the power of resilience and love as we
work to usher the light on to conquer the shadows that
plague our hearts and souls.

Threads of Truth

We weave our way
through love with gentle hands,
shedding our vulnerabilities.
Criss-crossing over emotions
like strands of thread coiled together,
intertwined between love, sorrow,
and strife.

Twisted threads of emotions
that lead us toward our truth,
where we can realize
our resilience to life and
commit our hearts to conquer
our fears, inspiring us to surrender
our lives to one another.

The Melody

To trust, to feel, to grieve, to love,
the melody of life becomes a fragile
symphony of the heart
where beautiful notes punctuate
the moments that bind us together
and define our journey.

In these melodic moments,
we create space for understanding,
space to triumph and space for despair.
Yet, in these spaces, we can rise in joy
and discover us within each other,
embrace our feelings and crack open
the door to our hearts, and defy
the limits of our existence.

Take My Hand

When the skies
shed tears of sorrow
where feelings
are captured
in a melancholy rain
take my hand
so our fingers
entwine together
forming a shelter
for our hearts
in doing so
our combined love
can continue to bind.

Love Unreturned

Your smile lit up my world, akin to the
sun breaking through the clouds,
where love filled my heart from that
very first moment. Believing that
you cared for me as much as I did you,
always hoping we had something
truthful and complete, only to be left
with cruel deception and painful lies,
finding myself lost in shattered illusions
and unreturned dreams.

The Echoes of Loss

Within the vacant chambers of my soul, the echoes of loss reverberate through the emptiness against a chorus of deep longing, seeking what we once held dear. And yet, in the night's stillness, I find solace.

My love, my lover, though no longer with me here on this earth remains endeared to me, transformed, transcended, to a realm I can visit in my sleep.

The memories we shared, the moments we cherished, linked by an unspoken truth, are a testament to our connection.

Time holds the key to unlocking the wisdom that heals me. To have loved and lost is not necessarily the end. It can be a new beginning. A journey guided by the very essence of remembrance. Through this journey, I can hold fast to the love we once shared and allow it to refresh and blossom again inside me.

Hushed Tones

Your soft tones
hum past my cheeks,
like soft kisses
caressing me
with your thoughts
where I find myself
drifting in love
with you as I
hum back.

The Voyage of Our Hearts

Hearts have navigated the unpredictable voyage,
steering across tumultuous waves between
love and heartache. Sharing vulnerabilities
anchored in the vast landscapes of emotions.
Where feelings can quickly become inflamed,
hidden beneath veils of anger that upend
rational thinking. Yet, despite the chaos,
hidden treasures can be discovered within
the foundation of the strength of love,
becoming the guiding beacon as we look
to heal the hurts from the past and find
the place where hope remains to join
the passion of shared intimacy, leaving
tenderness to sail together into the future.

I Give My Hand to You

In whispered dreams
of loss and sorrow
you clasp my hand
as we face tomorrow.
With love and trust
we forge our way
while moonbeams
kiss the night,
and light our way.

Intertwined

We stroll together, our fingers locked tightly
through life's tangled maze of emotions.
Feelings sway and flutter like the wings of a dove
to transform countless days within our garden of love.
With each footstep and passage, our hearts become
blended to overcome the obstacles and hardships waiting.
Yet, we triumph, a testament to the beauty
that belongs to us.

Family Ties

It is the unseen blood ties
that become the anchors that hold hearts together
by bonds forged deep.
A celebration of the unbreakable ties of unity
over shared stories around the table of belonging.
Where laughter, tears, and joy rise
to the love and tenderness of our connections,
and strife of turmoil, where we can find
a safe harbor in each other's arms.

The sanctuary of our relationships
becomes a refuge from generation to generation
of roots from our family tree's core of existence.
It is our epic tale of strength, perseverance,
and resilience transcending the bowels of our existence,
bounded together in the sanctuary
of our family's holy space.

Love's Garden

Let us walk together
through petals of trust
within the roots of honesty
deep and robust.

Hearts filled
with whispered feelings
and gentle caresses
like morning dew
tenderly sowing seeds of love
so our love can flourish
where honesty has grown.

Jacalyn Eyvonne

Jacalyn Eyvonne

Lessons from the Sun

As the sun rises,
to set the night ablaze
it sheds light
on the hate that
wounds us in so many
twisted ways.
The glow of light
brings revelation
giving sight to the
golden hues of truth.
Where we brave
the fog of chaos
that hides behind
smokescreens of
a blackened moon.

Bonded Battleground

I hear the war cry of the ancestors
bonded on the battleground.
Standing together side by side
inspiring us to merge our hearts
with the balm of the compassion
that lies beneath our feet.

To armor ourselves and swaddle
our spirits in the warmth of love
of one another as we prepare for
a war cry, loud and harsh, where we
overcome the murmurs of discord,
the blistering heat of hate and
march across the land together.

Tattered Soul

Nothing leaves
an emptiness
greater than
the hunger
that eats away
at your soul
when restrained
by the stained minds
of those insidious faces
that penetrate society
casting people aside
because of skin color.

Guardians Fight

Lives trampled
by oppressive feet
struggling to
press forward
from the backward
forcing of our freedoms.
Beneath deep despair
we fight the fight
against the grueling
harsh guards of equal rights.

Beneath The Loathing

Lives twist beneath
the chaos of loathing
thriving across lands
like a parasitic disease
feeding upon the embattled.
Those of us tinted
in pigment and hues,
cling to the hope that
continues to force us
into despair as we face
challenges from racist taunts
once dormant, now spiraling
within restless hate.

Shadows of our past meld
with the reawakened parallels
that continue to seek to
tear us apart.
We ready ourselves for
those moments of reprieve
from the bluster of hatred
so we can muster together
our strength to seek justice.

A Child's Cry

Wounding words cut deep into the soul
of a child torn in two when venomous
tongues spew hostility because someone
is different in their eyes.

There is a darkness in those so cruel to cause
suffering because of the shape of one's eyes
or the color of their skin. Piercing young
spirited hearts that only want to be youthful and play.

Where are all the protectors of innocence?
Where are the common goals of creating a world,
where love prevails over hate and children
can be free to be themselves?

Prayers to all the tiny souls
seated within the bowels of sadness,
corners of suffocating, narrow-mindedness.
Pray now before it is all too late.

Shadows of Fear

A little heart races beneath the canvas of darkness
where nightmares are born and monsters
roam as violence plagues slumber.

This should not be a child's reality,
waking up from dreams of news cycles,
echoes that have become commonplace,
where children worry about guns instead of grades,
and the sanctuary of the classroom
becomes spaces for learning how to avoid shooters.

Close your eyes and hope for a world
where the fire of hate is extinguished
and peace is the anthem that unites.
Where justice shines like the morning sun,
and shadows of fear no longer define your dreams.

Crumbling Structures of Society

Judgment blurs without trial or jury,
voices repressed for words and opinions.
While those with wealth keep the privilege,
regulate the faith of others by controlling,
holding on to the power in a crumbling world
as the underprivileged of society are slowly
and eventually devoured.

Stepped On

Skin color should not dictate fate.
Separation only serves to debase.
Racism has no place in society.
It tramples dignity and equality.

To Those Who Would Suppress Me

I refuse
to be treated
like a child
with disrespect
as if someone
you believe
to be ignorant.
I will not follow
behind you or
dance to your tune
simply because
you feel yourself
superior to
the shade of my skin.
I do not tap dance.
I do no mistrial shows.
I will not silence
myself for you.

Wildfire Rising

Angry hearts
spread hate like
wildfire rising.
Judging the color
of another's skin
ignoring the beauty
that shines
brightly within.

Prejudice boils
in the fiery flames
of rage as humanity
suffers and people
stand afraid.

We must speak up
even when unsure
of what to say
and stand strong
for progress
to come our way.

I Too Dream

I too dream
of brighter days
with hands clasped
we rise united.

Unchained in
a world mended
in justice and
kindness extends
in its purest form
across humanity.

Where hearts
are no longer
clad in despair.
and we all rise
side-by-side
together.

Ignite the Light

One drop of
kindness can
become a
tiny spark
a glint of light
the ripple that
defeats darkness
and the murky
waters of hate.

I Am the Holiday

I push forward
in the belief
that one day
change will
come my way.
Despite the hate
and negative vibes
I will endure
and celebrate me.

Rampage

Racism rampages in ugly form
discrimination has become the norm,
where unfair judgment spirals
in contempt of skin shade hues
with no sensitivity to one's value
or due.

The Weight of Hatred

The snarl of razor-edged hatred
defaces and burdens those
who only want to live their lives.

Constrained by the pain of word shackles
that repeatedly hold them in harm's way.
Words designed to smolder and steal away
the grace of hope in the souls of the many
targeted by the corrupt.

When Colors Collide

Invisible chains of unending lies divide humanity,
creating narrowminded visions of colors that collide,
segregating hearts and silencing cries.

Through a grotesque prism, we see a country
damned by its denial of fair reconciliation
and empathy due to skewed worldview vibes.

The Flowers in the Field

I will not go back to the cotton field
where sinister reign was the source
of so much black anguish and pain,
set against beautiful crops
of white decorative flowers,
lies a note to the tortured history
of hands that picked cotton,
with bleeding sores, weary souls
lived in bondage and toil.

I rise above the snide remarks
that scream, "Go pick some cotton,"
echoes falling from lips
that mock shadows of a brutal
past while tears of reminders
flow within the realities representing
our nation's story of gentle blooms
across land cursed by sorrow and pain,
roots of flowering that we will not forget.

Sometimes I wonder, do you hear what you say?
Do you see the pain it inflicts day by day?
Lashing out with hate-filled venom,
do you understand the weight of your words
as your language attempts to return us to slaves?

I will not go back to the cotton field,
to history's tortured stains of justice denied,
where racism flourished amid stolen lives.

Bigotry and hatred will not hold me back
from hearing the voices of those
who sang of freedom and love
as they fought to break the chains
of their oppression.
I rise with the strength of my ancestors
standing behind my back,
continually reminded of the painful past
where the cotton flower bloomed.

No, WE won't go back!

Still Black

My dark skin
cannot
be ignored.
It has become
a battle cry
for the dignity
and respect
that I am always
trying to achieve.
Yet I continue
even when
the result is
always the same
because in life
I remain black.

HOMELESSNESS

AS THE
HOMELESS
CONTINUE
TO FACE
LIFE'S
CRUELTY

CHAPTER 3

Haunting Lullaby

A sullen beast prowls amid empty bellies
in the cold, concrete jungles where hunger lies.
Silent and wretched pangs compose
a haunting symphony — a dark lullaby.

Cold Pavement

Where is the love
for the less fortunate?
Those who are vulnerable,
shrouded in abandonment,
desperate yet ignored,
left to be invisible,
to survive with only
cardboard in hand.
Where is the love?

Hunger on the Streets

When children
are food deprived,
and bellies grumble,
tear-filled eyes
beg for a bite to eat.
Urgent cries ring
from far away
as hunger pangs
hide in plain sight,
while we lament,
"How charity begins at home."
But what about those who roam?
Lost children
of families without
money or power
who walk streets
day and night
on empty stomachs.
No sustenance in sight.
Hoping for one
morsel of food,
one bite.

Shattered Dreams

Fingers clutched together tight,
shivering from the cold, dark of night.
A collective fight binds those without homes.
Broken spirits soar through shattered dreams,
together as they weather the extremes.

While They Feast

Those privileged few lay blind,
feasting high as millions starve.
The guttural cries of hunger
unveil the stories of hopelessness.
While the darkness whispers,
"Hunger — cruel and bold."

Entitled to Nothing

Suffocating cities
full of empty hearts
crowded with
emptied pockets,
and fractured dreams.
Societies invisible
housed in tented spaces,
surrounded by
silenced screams.

Absent-minded leaders,
deaf to their cries,
selfish turning
of a blind eye.
Hunger grows,
hope fades,
only statistics
left to be displayed
and filed away.

The Face of Our Fear

Tattered clothes worn with age,
shopping carts pushed by tired feet,
the weight of weariness lines faces,
protecting found possessions,
a chest of treasures on wheels
carrying all that they own.

The world looks past the unkept
raggedness and humbled beds
of cardboard covered in dirty blankets
soiled in tears.

Despair fills the hearts of the ignored,
when passing footsteps remain blinded
to their plight, afraid to see them,
fearful of the possibility of their own
reality.

Vanished paycheck, ruthless landlord,
a trajectory of tragedies can steal away
lives living one month from the misfortune
of cardboard protection from rain.
Removing the blinders might cause the
passersby to see themselves.

Tales of An Unjust Society

Cries of hunger
linger everywhere.
Poverty grips
the struggling
trying to survive.
To stay afloat
as inequities
remain alive.
Disparaged
in a country
on a downward
power dive.

A Simple Smile

She reflected a toothless grin stretched across
a soiled and tattered face. Her tininess
made me worry about her being on the streets.
How did she survive?
How did she maneuver throughout the night?

The dangers of the streets are unblurred.
I can feel its peril between brisk paces,
purse clutched tightly, keys in hand,
just in case I must blow my whistle,
or point the can of mace attached to my keychain,
at a stranger's face. Yet, despite my fears,
something about this woman caught my eye.

I don't know why I smiled at her or what made me
look in her direction; maybe it was the scar
slashed across her face. But I smiled,
and she smiled back as though our smiles
opened a pathway to another world,
where a beam of light connected us at that moment.

She became more than just a woman on the street
but a person with a story to tell. A fighter, a survivor
who was a reminder of the beauty felt from a simple
smile even in the darkest times

Shhhhh

Ruptured
battered
spirits crushed
leaders offer a
dismissive hush.
Collective failure
neglected duties
as the homeless
continue to face
life's cruelty.

A Dirge of Sorrows

A chorus of cries,
a lament of sorrows,
for those whose lives
become trapped in
hopeless tomorrows.

An empty stomach,
a vacant stare,
a cry for help
that goes unshared.

No one to fight
or stand in their corner,
injustice against those
who are poorer.

Abandoned By Society

Empty promises for better days
yet on every street corner, the pleas
of people without homes go unheard.
Lost in the noise of forgotten nights,
faced with continued roaming and
lives deterred.

Unwanted outcasts on sidewalks
sleeping in the cold, unsheltered
on park benches or makeshift sheds
where rats claw in the night,
as cries for help go ignored,
forced to hold on to unreachable dreams,
amid indifference and political schemes.

Becoming shadows that haunt society
blinded by material gain where leaders
boast of ineffective programs and legislative games,
the cruelty of a country's collective behaviors
only distributes promises of uncertainty,
and shameful fiascos and failures.

When Walls Close In

Facing the storm
of a looming eviction,
comes the unwelcome
challenge of stacked boxes
and family possessions piled high.
With no place to go, once happy lives,
forced to leave behind memories
within walls that once comforted,
walls now barren, rooms empty
of hope replaced with only reminders
from nail holes that once held
images of joy, to holding
unwavering fears of the unknown.
What shall they do without a roof or walls?

The truth of their circumstances bitterly stings.
The thought of homelessness becomes a test of fate.
Tears flood as the family clings to hope,
praying for a miracle to come.

Market of Greed

An open-air market of purveyors
where political greed masks the complex roles
of the hardened hands that disregard
what so many need.

Cloud of Struggle

Howling winds travel
across the night
like a lost child's cries
beneath a bruised
midnight sky.
A man without a bed
or roof stands under
a never-ending cloud
of struggle.
Hope becomes weary,
when wishing away
the pain of troubles
while trying to survive.

Let Us Light Up the Night

Poverty is too often an unavoidable fate,
for those living paycheck to paycheck
or with little food on their plates.
The inequalities of the world
are clear to see.

Misfortune of those in need
effects both you and me.
Loss of lives causes hope to fade,
as the poor go hungry and the rich
flourish more each day.

Justice must stand together in the fight
against poverty-stricken despair.
Let us light up the night against discrimination,
encouraging equality and fairness everywhere.

Do More

Do more than sing a song
for the class of people
living on the margins
of society.

Do more than offer
'Thoughts and prayers,'
while families cling
desperately to life's edge
after losing a loved one.

Do more for those
who struggle each day
to make ends meet.

Do more than watch
weary-eyed faces beg in the
streets without hope or options.

Do more for those caught
in the endless cycle of poverty
and dreary realities.

Do more.

Jacalyn Eyvonne

AGEISM

In a house that once bustled with life, only the sound of echoes remain where walls that once offered comfort surround and suffocate the air with the loneliness of a person who now sits Alone.

CHAPTER 4

Jacalyn Eyvonne

Twilight's Testament

Twilight does not fade with age,
I am in my sun's brightest zenith.
I tower, gifted by the winds of wisdom,
shadowed by the knowledge of knowing.

The echoes of my yesteryear softly resound,
a blend of joy and shadows from my life
filled with my elder tales and secrets.
The wrinkles are a testament to the
battles I have fought and won.

In these eyes, afire - is the strength of
my faith. Age is not a burden of shame
but a source of my sagacity.

Wisdom Vessel

As the sands of time flow past the years,
and fall swiftly from grasp, let not the lines
upon my brow become a trembling voice
of silent despair, nor a crumpled form
of weakness, distilling the fiery sage
that glows beneath my skin.

I sway to share my embers of stories,
that have traveled with me over the years.
Fragments of life that rise above any loss
of self and grip me with the gifts amassed,
bound inside the fibers of this enduring
wisdom vessel.

Even Though the Light Still Shines

Discrimination does not discriminate.
It wavers across race, body, and sex.
It attacks hearts that have turned the pages of life,
unable to escape nature's process.

Ageism rears its ugly head despite the fountain
of wisdom or years of experience or skills.
Regardless of whether you are an embodiment
of perseverance and grace, where your light
continues to burn brightly within.

Beauty in the Aging Sun

Do you hear it?
The clock ticking away
our precious moments
with every passing day.

Celebrate a life of toil,
and years of arduous work,
the wealth of stories left unsung
to share with those who come to hear.

Let age be just a number
as you seek the beauty of life
left to be celebrated, to bask
in the sunlight of gratitude,
shining bright across your years.

In The Shadow of Loneliness

In a house that once bustled with life,
only the sound of echoes remains.
Where walls that once offered comfort
surround and suffocate the air
with the loneliness of a person
who now sits alone, each ticking second
stealing away a bit more of life.

Memories of past days of laughter and smiles,
once companions are now only thoughts
and shadows that grow and bring tears
as the sun slowly sets in a home
where a heart fades from being alone.

Quiet of the Night

She feels him at night, lying in bed beside her.
A phantom arm around her waist,
a gentle kiss on her cheek.
She turns to whisper into the stillness.
"I miss you."

The lonely hours stretch out like desert sands,
bittersweet memories of daily life of the years
living with a man who was her rock,
left to journey past horizons without him.

Ageism Takes Its Toll

When a society
no longer sees your value
as your beauty fades
like a flower
in the winter snow.
Lines show your age,
as wrinkles and the gray
creep in faster each day.
Aging becomes the
unwelcomed guest
in spaces where people
base worth on physicality
rather than on what
truly matters,
the beauty that lies
beneath the fray.

Without

Life speeds by,
and the world goes on.
Without him, she stands
frozen in her loss.

Comforted by well-meaning friends,
sounds of words seem like far-away echoes,
meaningless and trite when you've lost
the life of someone meaningful to you.

"I'm so sorry."
"I'm praying for you."
"My condolences."
"You are in my prayers."

Only to scream aloud and tell
the world of the pain you feel,
the sorrow you carry in your heart.
Worries about the unknown terrain
that stretches before you.
Unready to accept life without
your soulmate by your side.

His loss stirs within your head.
Missing the legacy of the joy and
the years shared.

The Weight of Age

In seasoned years, when shadows
creep throughout the walls of night,
a weary man holds memories close to his heart.
With trembling hands and feeble breath,
he ponders life. He ponders death.

His grown children have flown the nest
to seek their purpose, to chase their stars.
His wife's hand no longer beside him to hold,
no one to hear the stories once told.
Alone, he sits, a man both saddened and old.

His worth now questioned by youthful eyes,
his once bustling life has passed him by,
he feels the weight of age as scorn,
resigned to be alone, to be forlorn.

Grandparents

Grandparents become guardians of time,
epic lives, where wisdom imparts the
well-lived presence of a consummate life.
Sharing the footpaths of days traveled,
validated by the lines on their brow,
they hold both insight and knowledge,
becoming the bridge that connects
the past to the present, to be honored
in all their glory, for they are the
guardians of history to pass on their stories.

Aging With Joy

Savor each moment
inhaling the years,
embracing joy while
moving non-stop
through pain knowing
that you are the blessing,
passing through dark
moments and sad days.

We cannot stop
the passage of time,
but we can step into
the future like
a gift-wrapped present,
never to be taken
for granted.

A Love Entwined

Love lies bound
in the deep of night.
Hands draped across
one another's bodies,
holding tight to the
decades of marriage.
Flesh wrinkled and
weakened by age,
no longer in their
earthly prime.
Yet their infinite love
remains forever entwined.

The Woman

A vibrant beauty aged by time,
peers at the wrinkles
that show the passage of years.
She stares in the mirror,
wondering who the
stranger is that stares back.

Touching her face with hands
tired from hard labor,
her back stiff with age.
Silvery pallets of white hair
drape across her face.

Questioning if those who once
called her pretty, speak of her
vanished beauty with disdain.
Was it worth all the years
striving to look good?
To only turn into what looks
back at you today.

Yes.

Lonely Hours

The clock ticks on
with painful persistence.
Motions without meaning,
ticking away the remaining
seconds of life, as memories
hold tight to words like
love and hope, and things
seen and shared to join in
the passageway of white light
where sleep meets longing.

The timekeeper becomes
a constant reminder
of the passing days
until hearts meld together
once more restored in love.

A Love Letter

His aged face, painted with grief, lay bare
as she, his wife, softly embraced his hand.
Her whispers are unplanned.

I see your lines, those rivers deep,
I feel your pain; I know the secrets you keep.
But you must see the strength and fire
that will not die, your eyes belie.

We have both grown old, but strong we stand.
You have built our life with hardened hands.
You are my map of victory in endless ways,
the love of my life to whom I give all my praise.

I love you.

Stage of Life

Once youthful,
nimble legs
now stricken
with arthritis,
movement
becomes a luxury
surrounded by
the impatient
and uncaring
who do not believe
older adults
should have a
comforting place
in this life.

When The Mirror Haunts

It happens on days
when my reflection
looks back at me,
becoming a haunting,
unbearable sight.
When I hate what I see,
hating what looks
back from the
mirror world at me.

Wondering where
did the past go?

Not seeing myself
as I had for so long,
but finding myself looking
into the eyes of a stranger.

Dance

I awake dancing to the stillness
that I live within. A life empowered,
leaping in my liberation,
to explore new things
and unlock life's hidden surprises.

The adventures that wait around
each bend, lead me on an exploration,
grabbing moments as I age
with hope and grace and
the wisdom that shines brightly
over the wear and tear of my years.

I dance because I am empowered
by the acceptance of my years,
igniting me to want to live for me.

Don't Be Afraid to Live

Spirits never fade
but become wiser
as life's journey
crosses into later years
of new beginnings.
A precious gift to cherish
is the nectar that comes
with the marathon of life.
Where memories carry blessings
for those who chase the sunshine
and reach for the sky with grace,
living the sweet years of life
to the fullest
because growing old
is not a curse.

Strength in the Aging Sun

Living the vigor
of years fulfilled,
the streams of life
quietly amass.
Below sunset hues,
beneath the beckon
of twilight nights.
Behold the wisdom,
the beauty formed
in God's eternal gift
of a life lived long.

Internal Hourglass

The sands of your internal hourglass run quietly,
a slow dwindle with each passing day as the outer shell
of humanity ages, and the weariness of life shows in the
essence of lines that slowly settle over your face. Once
richly colored strands of hair lose their vibrant flare,
inevitably fading to clouds of gray heaven as days become
shorter, memories and focus become sluggish as the
sands slowly dwindle one by one.

When A Youthful Heart Remains

It is easy to forget you've aged
like a sweet vintage wine
when your heart still thinks
it's a baby grape on the vine.

CHOICE

AFRICAN AMERICAN BOOKS

Chained
Minds

The minds
that once
beheld
bright skies
and dreamt
of winged
tomorrows,
inquisitive eyes
narrowed, now
plagued by
ignorance and
sorrow in forsaken
chambers of knowledge

CHAPTER 5

Jacalyn Eyvonne

A World of Whitewashed Books

In a world
where words hold no meaning,
the artist's paintbrush
replaced by a sponge,
and their inkwells,
overflow with bleach.

We bear witness to
whitewashed books,
where forlorn stories
lay in slumber.
Tales of love and courage
resigned to the
abyss of silence.

A child whispers,
"Where have my books gone?"
A mother asks,
"What have we become?"
As they both gingerly turn
the pages of books that
have become the ghost
of forgotten words.

Edited Out

Like silent fall leaves
lives quieted with the stroke of a pen
and screams of, "Don't say gay!"
By lifeless thieves devoid of heart.
You are
Penciled out
Crossed-out
Edited
Erased
Striking lines through humanity
as though they were nothing.

Chained Minds

The minds
that once beheld
bright skies and dreamed
of winged tomorrows,
inquisitive eyes narrowed,
now plagued by ignorance
and sorrow in forsaken
chambers of knowledge.

Vanished Identity

In quiet steps
my spirit stalled
like a dancer
close to death
gasping at
shapeless forms
devoid of identity
and vivid memories
of me have become
phantoms.

This is how I feel
when you attempt
to erase me.

Love Knows No Gender, No Color

Until the day comes when acceptance annuls hate,
we will entwine our fingers, share a kiss,
and prevail in faith.
Past glaring eyes and poisonous berates,
our love will be unbroken as we live open without
boundaries in place.
We shall not hide our continued love for each other,
wrapped in full pride, hand in hand.

Freedom To Choose Is Hers

Her right, regardless of the
wild flailing of freedoms removed,
hate traversing countrywide
penetrates worse than the sting
of an epidural needle piercing
the spinal nerve.
Her right to bear a child or not.
Her fate determines when and how.
Her body, my body, matters not.
Choices to make one's own decision
fall upon her, not men who have never
known the feeling of cradled life
floating within an amniotic womb.
Raise your voices in unison.

The thin wall of choice to control your body
… is yours.

War of the Whisperers

They say it begins with a whisper,
murmurs of malice, where a kernel
of venom seeps beneath the ugliness
of individuals as hatred festers and
attacks the young, filling their days with
sadness like shadows eclipsing the sun.

To deny a child's life, their struggle to
understand themselves, ban differences,
and scorch them with harmful words
fueled by rage. You create a fortress
of pain that clouds them in despair.

We cannot allow children to wither away.
We cannot break their spirits like glass.
The violence of our words becomes the
assault on innocence that once blossomed.
A child's difference should not be a curse
felt by you.

The Babel of Voices

A true sign of cultural richness
is the sound of the different languages,
all spoken in a unified den of humanity
to present vibrant shades of sounds
and hues that tell this country's story.

Target of Their Rage

Constantly judged
for being different
for not fitting in
as if conforming
is the only way to win
hated for misjudged
perceptions of me
not for me being me.
Living in a world
where every aspect
of my being
is challenged.

My choices, my beliefs,
my gender, my identity
seem always to be a reason
for society's depravity.

Don't Dim Your Light

Don't let the haters bring you down;
their vitriol does not define your crown.
You shine bright in your own way,
with hues of color on full display.
Stares and taunts may follow you around,
but don't let their hate bring you down.
You are a gem meant to shine,
so let your light sparkle, and you'll be fine.

When Dictate Is the Rule

We tether children to untruths,
as history eradicates all depictions
of whom they are.

Told to obey, attempts to conquer their minds.
To deprive them with the dishonesty
of dogma, deceit, and one-sided truths.

White Lies

On the shelf, a tomb of lies,
hidden hues thinly disguised.
Once vibrant colors of history
danced and sang on shelves,
revealing stories of hope and shame.

The souls of heroes' past are gone.
Whispered songs are ashen dawns.
all painted white, all stories wrong.

No Libraries Left

Will the future be days
of the last library?
Where we bid farewell
to hallowed halls
and troves of knowledge
that once cradled
our minds and dreams.

What happens in the absence
of these vaulted keepers?
Where wisdom burns,
tossed out to become
driftwood of stories erased
and no longer told.

Young minds no longer
wonder through vibrant aisles
of truth, and histories are
no longer beacons of hope
as accurate accountings
become lost legacies of the past
to fade like whispers.

Victory

Life can break a heart
when you open yourself
to a world that can wound.
Yet, within us lies secrets
that hold the beauty dwelling
inside each of us.
The power of choice,
the ability to endure,
quells feelings of brokenness
amid our most profound sadness
where strength thrives
and we gain victory over our fears.

Political Rule

Bans, like vengeful Gods, wield swords of despair,
as the biased political rule silences the voices
that ignores the cries of women left with uncertain
futures.

Only to lurk beneath modern-day shackles
formed to restrict a woman's choice,
beneath the weight of laws where her body,
her future and her sovereignty all crumble
to bureaucracy as state decrees erase independence.

Leaving only shadows of a past now rendered mute.
Shrouded in uncertainty that suffocates,
and strips away her right to choose.

Embrace Your Individuality

The world can be a cruel, constant battlefield
where you must fight for acceptance, fight to find your
place. But what happens when society refuses to welcome
you when you are labeled as different, inferior, or
someone to be feared?

Discriminated against only because of your skin color
or who you choose to love, even though love knows no
bounds.

The weight of hate, the force of rage, can be unbearable.
Leaving you with the feeling of walking through a
minefield, never knowing when the ground will give way
beneath your feet.

Trying hard not to give up hope and not let bigotry define
you. Knowing that you are more than the labels placed
upon you and that you have the right to celebrate love in
all its forms.

I Want Grandbabies

I beam smiles through rose-colored conviction
each time I utter hopeful words to my son,
"I want grandbabies." Yearning for that festive day,
to welcome and hold tight to a new life
and sing a soothing lullaby
while pressing soft kisses to a little cheek.
Until his words pierced my heart
like an arrow driven deep. "Mom," he said,
"Had it not been for abortions, you would have three."

His grief penetrated through the words he voiced,
and I felt a torturous pain, yet as a woman
whose womb has long done its bidding,
it is still our body, our choice, and our pain.
Regardless of the beliefs of others,
irrespective of the ache of disappointment.
Including my disheartening probing
and the bemoaning because there will be
no grandbabies from my son.

Choice.

Jacalyn Eyvonne

.

HOPE

CHAPTER 6

Jacalyn Eyvonne

Healing Reflection

Beneath the turmoil and strife,
A silent strength lies deep inside.

In times of great despair,
one's inner power must rise
to face life's struggles and toils
and seek peace inside yourself.

Reflections where minds craft
solutions, through hurt and
oppressive rife to delve into
our emotions and find the strength
to choose to start again.

If We Only Speak It Out Loud

Feelings easily
paralyze a person
infected by the
powerlessness
of the oppression
that suffocates lives.
And yet, together,
we can rise to
create change
when we stand
in tandem
side-by-side,
in chorus as one.

The Lighthouse of Hope

A country
embroiled in
the breath
of distress,
the light of hope
still hovers
and dances
across the dimness
of raging winds
clamoring
over our lives
like angry waves.
To wade
through days
where untarnished
truth is still more
powerful than
the pounding sea,
to ferry ourselves
into a brighter future.

Reverie of the Forgotten Ones

Whispers flow across the night,
past children living within the shadows' plight,
where cracks reveal the clay beneath,
the broken masks of melanin grief.

Faint echoes bounce through saddened hearts,
their voices rise through tear-drenched eyes
and discrimination runs rampant amid chaotic lies.

The trembling hands of those rebuffed within
the bold injustices endured, their entire world collided,
forced to deal with the hate ignited.

Blackhearts erupt within the gloom of twilight,
to savor the aura of conquering the night,
planting feet of clay, with newfound grace,
to stride forward to mend this broken space.

Silenced Voices

Stories unspoken
turn to dust,
hearts trampled
and battered
in time can rust,
our forgotten whispers
dance in the dark,
hidden behind
our fear-tarnished marks.

The world has taught
us to close our minds,
silencing our thoughts
with stifling binds.
Suppressed are the voices
of change unreformed,
when the fire of hope
is challenged,
yet will not be scorned.

Journey of Two Hearts

A love potion of perfected moments,
untamed desire caught in time,
in droplets of pure emotions.
Sealed in a bottle, kept afloat,
and carried by the ebb tides gentle swell.

Two hearts sealed in love,
intertwined to ride waves of destiny,
journeying together, patiently awaiting
the moment when destiny unfolds and
the bottle of love washes upon a distant shore.

As the magic of the elixir is released, the holder
of the bottle will be touched by destiny's kiss,
unmatched in kindness and generosity of the heart,
and molded to bind with another, a gift to the finder
of the humbled vessel of love plucked from the sea.

It's Okay to Cry

Tears are the language of emotion
Expressions of pure joy or sadness
Flowing from within, cleansing away
Sorrows to bring forth a sense of release
Becoming unbidden reminders
Of our humanity.

Around The Front Back

Sometimes the road
takes you around
the front back,
where you must look
behind you into the past
before moving forward.
Reviewing behaviors
and mistakes.
Understanding history
and the roads traveled,
in order not to repeat
the horror that plagues
and seeds hatred.
Looking ahead is important,
but looking behind you
is revealing.

Memories

Our loved ones
Become the
Warm embrace
Enveloping you
In the comfort
Of their love.
With each
Gentle droplet
Of soft rainfall,
Each breeze
Whispering past
Reminders
Of their presence
Memories that
Nestle within
So you will
Always know
They are nearby.

Hope's Flourish

From the depths of pain and sorrow
Where dark clouds obscure minds
Seeds of hope take root and grow.

The birth of a flower blooms past despair
New buds struggling to survive through days
Of sadness, anger, or rage, moments fraught
With pain lends itself to the power of strength
Flourishing within each of us.

To triumph and overcome adversities,
becoming a rosebud to flower, to rise again.

Unbroken

Upon the cracked and fractured earth,
the poison of disdain spews desperate
and contrived beliefs to force the fate
of others into a well of deception.

Rivers weep with tears as the drumming
of racism resounds loudly in attempts to swing
the pendulum back in time, efforts to keep us
immersed within broken shells of the past.

Our whispers grow with tales to tell of history,
dreams shattered, and lives impaled beneath
the lies, still our humanity continues to be unveiled.

Our Souls Revealed

By the moon's silken touch
or the sun's warming glow,
the lines of our stories will forever unfold.
The harmony of our virtue unhidden,
our souls and hearts revealed.
We will remain etched in the annals of history,
where strength will inspire and uplift the people
as we rise from the mire to the top of the steeple.

You Are in There

If you are ever lost
in the darkness
of your despair
reach beyond
the shadows
of your soul,
and grab
the light
that will
make you hold.

Homebound

We have watched the ebony sky unfold,
heard the winds sing the songs of our ancestors,
murmurs of grievance feed the anger
over widespread wrongs.

Far from our fatherland, we live in a maze
of unanswered questions, wandering deep
within our dreams, seeking our heritage,
sleepwalking inside visions of a world
where our humanity is celebrated.

We are exhausted melanin travelers
in pursuit of lives beyond uncertainty,
searching for a haven where we can look
upon the stars in peace and leave behind
the flow of tears that overwhelms our hearts.

Beneath our feet, we stand on the souls
of those who gave us birth, the answers
embedded within the soil begin in the
roots of our lineage, in the depths of the sea
that leads us back to our motherlands.

When Echoes Tremble

Old echoes tremble
beneath midnight's cloud,
awaken, melanin, strong, and proud.
Join hands in camaraderie!
Unleash the whirlwind of unity.

A New Dawn

Akin to the Phoenix
rise from the ashes
of destruction
where pain and strife
give birth to the light
that shines to brighten
the night
emerging from the
depths of darkness
to lead the way
from the cinders
of rage and hate
to a place where
hope and grace
radiates in every
direction far and near.

The Shape of Our Reality

The issue of race can
be sensitive to some
but seeing each other
through the lens of history
can help us understand
the shape of our realities.

The Broom's Embrace

With every swish
of the broom's firm bristles,
she sweeps away unwanted
bits of her life,
casting out sleepless nights,
memories of broken relationships,
forcing out the hurt and pain,
anger, and resentment,
clearing away all the things
that made her cry.

The handle gripped tightly
as she whisks back and forth,
her movements are deft,
her pace grows stronger
with each stroke,
and sadness
slowly begins to dissipate.
The broom sways,
dancing across the floor,
she is liberated in her process
of healing, uncaged
from the chains of the past.

As she collects the dust,
she tosses it out into the trash,
her ceremony now concluded,
leaving her with the strength
and resilience to rise
above tomorrow's challenges,
to sweep a new chapter into her life,
bidding goodbye to all she
wants to leave behind.

Jacalyn Eyvonne

About The Author

Jacalyn Eyvonne became part of a poetic duo as co-Poet Laureate for the City of Vallejo, CA., for the term of January 1, 2024 – December 31, 2025, along with writer Kathleen Herrman. Jacalyn immediately embraced the opportunity to weave connections and immerse herself in the beauty of Vallejo's rich and diverse culture.

An Academy of Art University/Motion Picture and Television graduate, producing over three hundred films. Jacalyn offers a unique blend of creative expression through poetry, writing, photography, and film. At the core of every project lies her passion for inspiring, conveying messages through storytelling, and celebrating diversity.

She is the former founder of "In The Company of Poets" magazine. The current founder/director of the Monologues and Poetry International Film Fest and the International KidsNFilm Festival. Her published books include "I Am Not An Inconsequential Word-Poetry/Memoir. Venting To Verse–How To Turn Anger Into Poetry." And the short-story collection "Strange Things Happen at Midnight.

As a mother, Jacalyn writes for moms and dads rearing children, living with unsettled fear because of skin color, choice, or simply who they choose to be. As a Black woman, she has experienced oppression and marginalization due to race, gender, and age. Recognizing the continuing struggles has led her to serve as a mentor for youth and a role model for those trying to carve out their paths.

Jacalyn understands the importance of activism for greater inclusion of people who look like her and those confronted with similar barriers. She advocates through art and word poetizing as she continues to journal about hurtful words and unkind people.

Jacalyn thrives off connecting with her readers and would love your thoughts and feedback. Don't hesitate to drop her a line at **author.jacalyneyvonne@gmail.com**

Books By Jacalyn Eyvonne
Available on Amazon
"I Am Not An Inconsequential Word."
"Venting To Verse – How To Turn Anger Into Poetry."
"The World of Black and Words"

Coming November 2024
Youth Poetry Letters Anthology
"Dear Feelings, Deep Thoughts, and Me"

A joint project between Jacalyn Eyvonne and Kathleen Herrman, in partnership with VTA, Vallejo Teaching Artists.
For more information about submitting your poetry letter, visit www.youthpoetryletters.com
poetry@youthpoetryletters.com